ACADEMY FOR ROBLOX PROS

GAME ON!

AF585216

AN UNOFFICIAL ROBLOX GRAPHIC NOVEL

Scholastic Australia
An imprint of Scholastic Australia Pty Limited
PO Box 579 Gosford NSW 2250
ABN 11 000 614 577
www.scholastic.com.au

Part of the Scholastic Group
Sydney • Auckland • New York • Toronto • London • Mexico City • New Delhi
Hong Kong • Buenos Aires • Puerto Rico

Published by Scholastic Australia in 2024.
Written and illustrated by Louis Shea.
Text and illustrations copyright © Scholastic Australia, 2024.

The moral rights of Louis Shea have been asserted.

All rights reserved. No part of this publication may be reproduced or transmitted in any form or by any means, electronic or mechanical, including photocopying, recording, storage in an information retrieval system, or otherwise, without the prior written permission of the publisher, unless specifically permitted under the Australian Copyright Act 1968 as amended.

A catalogue record for this book is available from the National Library of Australia

ISBN: 978-1-76129-966-7

Typeset in Extra Crunchy.

Printed in China by Hang Tai Printing Company Limited.

This product is made of material from well-managed FSC®-certified forests, recycled materials, and other controlled sources.

10 9 8 7 6 5 4 3 2 1 24 25 26 27 28 / 2

ACADEMY FOR ROBLOX PROS

GAME ON!

AN UNOFFICIAL ROBLOX GRAPHIC NOVEL

It's Monday morning, and as parents everywhere once again prepare to do battle with their slumbering children to wake them up for school, something strange (and unnatural) is happening in the houses of four Borelock's Academy students . . .

At Beatrice's house

KNOCK! KNOCK!

Good morning, Mum and Dad!

At Mitch's house

Time to get up! It's a beautiful day!

At Tash's house
No more sleeping in! You don't want to be late for work.
At Jai's house 
SNORE!
Wakey wakey! Breakfast is ready!

Don't take too long in the bathroom!

Your lunch is on the table. Don't be late for work!

MUM

DAD

Make sure you brush your hair before you leave.
I've put your report for work on the table so you won't forget it ... again!

BUS
STOP

Hey, guys! How was your weekend?
Long!
Soo long!
I'm just glad it's finally Monday!

It'd be so cool if school went all week long.

Yeah! No boring weekends to spoil it!

Look! Here comes the bus!

Yay! We'll be at school soon!

I can't wait to get there!

What have we got first?
Maths.
Woo-hoo!
Um ... Maybe we should keep it down a bit ... We're getting a few angry looks from the other kids.

Under the cold, resentful stares of their fellow students, Tash, Beatrice, Jai and Mitch walked excitedly into their school, Borelock's Academy.

Smiling, happy children on a Monday morning? Something is definitely not normal!

And things continue to get even stranger, as a shocked teacher sees her students discussing the merits of math ...
This is awesome! We can use trigonometry to calculate the angle needed, which will be so helpful in Roblo ... um ... other classes ...

Then, Beatrice's effort on the rope climb in sport blows the mind of the P.E. teacher—though in fairness, it's a pretty small explosion!
Woah! Go Bea!
My turn next!
What is going on?!
What can explain this disturbing behaviour?

What a great morning!
Sure was!
What shall we do for lunch?
Hmm ... What about some extra 'study'?
What a great idea!
Yeah, let's go 'study' in the computer lab.
Oh great, it's Roger. I guess you're here to 'study' too?
Study?! What are you losers on about?
COMPUTER LAB

We're trying to be subtle so no-one learns our secret!
Whatever! You dweebs worry too much!

Badges on!

Let the studying ...

... begin!
WELCOME, STUDENTS . . .

DEMY
FOR
ROBL
PROS
Oof!
TO THE ACADEMY
FOR ROBLOX PROS!

SCHOOL BADGES

So this explains the mystery of the happy students! Beatrice, Tash, Jai and Mitch each have a very special school badge that can transport them to the awesome, amazing, astounding, Academy for Roblox Pros. Here they become their avatar selves; Bee, Dash,

Play, Glitch and Fritz (Glitch's super-smart hair avatar).

Unfortunately, Borelock's biggest pest, Roger, also has one of these wonderful badges too. He becomes the avatar, Ogre—which matches his personality perfectly!

But, how did they come by these brilliant badges?

It all happened when Roger spilled his Super Slime Squishy on one of Mitch's genius inventions. The combination of Mitch's invention and the Super Slime Squishy created a portal into Roblox! The gang transported into the Roblox universe where they became avatar students at the Academy for Roblox Pros. After saving the school from the Warlock, the kids were presented with school badges so they can teleport into the Academy any time.

In the space of their school lunch break, they fit in a whole day of exciting, fun and occasionally dangerous lessons at the Academy for Roblox Pros. At the end of the Roblox day, they use their badges to transport themselves back to Borelock's.

It's great to be back!

Hey guys!

My talking avatar hair is back! Hi, Fritz!

CLUNK!

ZAP!

We need the laser pointed at 35 degrees. Quick, fire!

Back at Borelock's at the end of lunch ...

Ouch!

CLUNK!

BAM!

CRASH!

Why do I always land on my head?!

Watch it!

COMPUTER LAB

Well, another exciting day over for ...

COMPUTER LAB

Robloooh ...

Study!

Yeah ... Can't wait for more exciting study tomorrow ...
I think that's enough, Jai.

So what's on now?
Double history.
Ohhh! Why can't school be over already?!

But it wasn't over! And as the school day continued on and on . . . and on . . . Beatrice, Tash, Mitch and Jai tried to concentrate as their minds wandered. Dreaming (literally in Jai's case) of what adventures were in store for them at the Academy for Roblox Pros the next day.

After what seemed longer than the whole Roman Empire (which they were learning about), the bell finally sounded.

'That's it for the Romans!' said Mrs Fossil, their history teacher. 'But don't despair,' she continued, 'we'll be moving onto the Dark Ages next!'

'I think I just went through the Dark Ages in that lesson,' muttered Beatrice, as they slumped out of the classroom.

Can we go home now?
Nope, we've still got one lesson to go.

Ugh! Well at least it can't be as boring as double history ... What is it?
I think it's ...

BING!
Attention, students! Please make your way to the school hall for afternoon assembly.

There, there, Jai. You'll be all right.

PAT! PAT!

sob *sob*

I wonder what the assembly's for?

Everybody, settle down!

That's better! Now, I have some news for you ...

Oh great.

C'mon, Bea, it could be good this year.

But we always finish last!

10th Place

PARTICIPATION AWARD

I expect you all to try your hardest ...

... to carry on the fine tradition of success at Borelock's Academy.

BEST SLUG IN SHOW

RUNNERS RUNNERS RUNNERS UP

TURNING UP AWARD

Well, I'm glad that day's over! Can't wait for school tomorrow though!

Yeah!

Me too!

The inter-school comp might be OK this year ...

What are you talking about?! We always get bloxxed by the other schools!

We might do better this year. Maybe our extra 'study' will help us?

If there's a zombie battling tournament we'll definitely do OK!

The next day, at the Academy for Roblox Pros, the gang's first lesson is to each find and befriend a forest animal. A task that some are finding easier than others ...

Help! The world's upside-down!
Whoa, slow down, Shelley!
Wait up, guys!

That was awesome! I wish I could ride my unicorn everywhere!

We have to let them go back to the forest, Bee.

But, we've bonded ...

Aargh! No more bonding, you crazy bird!

Nom! Nom!

BING! BING!
There goes the bell. Race you back to school!

BiNG! BiNG!

ATTENTION STUDENTS: Please gather in the school hall for an assembly.

I wonder what Principal Blox is going to announce?

Hopefully he's extending the school day!

As always, we'll be competing against our good friends from Bloxford College and the Obby Academy. And this year, we have a new school competing ...

Please welcome Principal Limax from the newly founded Slimelox Institute.

Check out the new principal's outfit!

I know! And that hair and moustache! There's something familiar about him though ...

THE
ROBLOX
CUP

Which school's going to win the super-cool, Roblox Cup?!

Each year, The Academy for Roblox Pros, Bloxford College and the Obby Academy have battled it out in a series of challenges to see who'll take home the prestigious prize.

This year however, there's another school taking part in the fun, The Slimelox Institute. Lead by the mysterious and badly dressed Principal Limax, can the new school upset the mix and take home the trophy?

Later that day, back at Borelock's

Ah, yes! Beautiful! What a fine specimen!

Fat and juicy! You'll be perfect!

Compared to taking down that stupid Warlock and his smelly zombies ...

Huh?

... winning the Roblox Cup should be simple!

I don't know, Bea. I bet there's heaps of good avatars at the other schools.

Well, well, well! So those are the pesky kids that thwarted me last time!

I think they'll need watching so they don't spoil my plans again. Go, faithful zombie bunny! Keep an eye on them!
Hop!
Hop!

Right, my slimy friend. It's time to get you to your new home before the lunch break's over and all those horrible students return to class!

DANGER
BIO-HAZARD

KEEP OUT!

We're safe now! Hmm, what shall I call you, my beauty? Slimone ... Yes, Slimone Slug!
CLANG!

You have all the attributes of a fine leader! I shall make you the captain of my new school!

Take a seat, Slimone.
SQUELCH!

Now, let me turn on your computer screen ...

... And here's something to magnify your magnificent mind ...

Now go join your fellow students. And soon Roblox will be ...

MINE!!!

MWA!
HA!
HA!

Uh-oh! It seems Principal Borelock is back to his old tricks, and is about to cause some major trouble in the Roblox universe!

Having been foiled in his attempt to take over the Academy for Roblox Pros with his zombie army, he now has a new plan to wreak havoc!

In his guise as Principal Limax, he's set up a rival school, The Slimelox Institute, to take part in the Roblox Cup.

But can his school of super slimey slug avatars really cause that much trouble? Will Dash, Play, Bee, Glitch and Fritz be able to stop him again?

Is a super slug student a match for a human one (apart from Ogre)?

How much mischief can a green zombie bunny get up to? Only time will tell ...

The next morning, at the bus stop ...

I'm so excited! I could hardly sleep last night.

Me too! I dreamt we won the Roblox Cup!

I dreamt that I was being followed everywhere by a green rabbit.

You've got to stop eating pizza straight before bed, Jai!

But I didn't. Well ... maybe a few slices.

Hey, losers! Ready to be beaten by me in the Roblox Cup?!
TAXI

Morning, Roger. You do realise we're on the same team, right?

You wish! You're just scared you'll lose!

B-B-Bea! Its the green b-b-bunny in a taxi!
Lay off the pizza, Jai.

After a gruelling morning of Borelock's lessons, Mitch, Bea, Jai and Tash rushed to the computer labs to catch up on a bit of 'study'.

Pressing their special school badges, they are once again transported to the Academy for Roblox Pros.

'Ah, time for some real classes,' smiled Bee.

'Yep,' agreed Dash. 'I wonder what fun lessons we've got today?'

'As long as there's no bunnies involved, I don't care,' said Play, looking nervously around, just in case.

At that moment, an announcement echoed around the school: 'All students proceed to the assembly hall!'

'It must be something about the Roblox Cup!' said Fritz.

'I bet we get to find out what the different challenges are,' said Glitch. 'Let's go!'

There was a huge buzz of excitement as the gang joined the throng of avatar students heading towards the assembly hall.

ASSEMBLY HALL

But first, it's time to change into our customised competition outfits.

Nice!
Cool threads!

Now, each school has their own unique uniform for the games.

Bloxford College

Obby Academy

Slimelox Institute

Before we start, in the spirit of friendship—which is what these games are really about—let's take this opportunity to meet and mingle with avatars from the other schools.

Hey guys, how are you going? My name's Play. What's yours?

I am the one named Sylvester and this is our great leader, Slimone.

Cool. So, what's the deal with Slimelox? Sounds like a school for snails! Ha ... ha ... ha ... hmm ...

Just joking ... you know ... slime ... snails ...?
A joke. Ha. Ha.
Yes. Ha. Ha.

Um ... well ... good to meet you!

I think I can hear someone calling me ... I better be off. See you around!

Sheesh! Those Slimelox kids are a bit odd!

They hardly laughed at my jokes at all!

Seems pretty normal to me.

Look! Everyone's starting to head off. Let's go choose our comps!

THE ROBLOX CUP CHALLENGES

1. OBBY

Perfect! I know what I'm doing!

2. THE PUZZLER

Excellent! A challenge of mind over matter!

We have two of those!

3. FOREST FRIENDS
Yessss! All cute creatures love me!

4. THE RAD RACE
Oh! I was hoping it'd be a pizza eating competition. I guess car racing's almost as good!

5. TEAM EVENT
What's the team event?
They haven't said what it'll be.
Must be a surprise . . .
Team pizza eating?

I've got track and field training tomorrow before lunch, which will be a good warm-up for the Obby.

So, Tash will be competing in the first Obby ...

This is useful information, Bunny. You have done well!

SNATCH!
CHOMP!

We'll just have to organise some extra training for Tash tomorrow!
BURP!

Next day at Borelock's ...
Right, kids, Principal Borelock has said he wants you to train extra hard for the inter-school cross country event this year.

Just follow the flags and you shouldn't get too lost.

TOOT!

That's weird! The course has never gone out of the school grounds before ...

Um ... Anyone know where the flag's gone?

I think we should go back to school!

Oh no, the lunch bell! I've got to hurry!
DING! DING!

Huh?! The back gate's been locked.
RATTLE! RATTLE!

We can't get back into the school!
Cool!

I've got to get to the front gate! I can't miss lunch!

Give it a rest, Jai! It's not funny.

I'm not joking! I sa-

Look! It's Tash!

Oh no, she's stuck outside the gate!
No she isn't! Look at her go!

Quick, Tash! We're late!
What happened to you?
I'll tell you later. I've got a ...
MPUTER LAB

race to run!

What's the hold up, Blox?! We should have started already!
We're missing a student. We'll just wai-
START
I don't think so! Out of the way!
SHOVE!
WHAM!
GO

1ST CHALLENGE - OBBY

Principal Limax! That was uncalled for!
Hi, Principal Blox! Sorry I'm late!

Oh my! Isn't Dash fast! She's catching up already.

FINISH

Adversary approaching rapidly. We must block them so the leader can win.

OBBY WINNER IS:
SLIMONE, FROM THE
SLIMELOX INSTITUTE.

After the race, Dash made her way back to her friends.

'Awesome race, Dash!' beamed Fritz.

'Yeah, you were amazing!' agreed Bee. 'Coming from starting last and nearly winning!'

'I guess so,' replied Dash in a dejected voice, 'but I think I could've won. If only those Slimelox kids didn't get in my way.'

At that moment, there was a burst of laughter from behind them. Turning, they saw Principal Limax congratulating the Slimelox student who won the race.

'Ha ha! Excellent work! Thanks to your natural talents and my genius, the result was never in doubt.'

Principal Limax turned to look at Bee, Dash, Play, Glitch and Fritz. He was glaring at them, but a smile was creeping across his face.

‘Even the cheating attempts from those Academy for Roblox fools couldn’t stop you!’ he sneered. ‘Poor Slyvester and Slayla,’ he continued. ‘Being viscously attacked during the race. I will demand points be taken from their school! Where’s that blockhead, Blox?’

With one last sneer, Principal Limax marched off in search of Principal Blox.

‘Can you believe that?!’ said Play angrily. ‘He’s accusing you of cheating?! What a nerve!’

‘I know,’ replied Dash. ‘It was his students that tried to slow *me* down! I hope he doesn’t get me disqualified.’

‘No chance!’ said Bee. ‘Principal Blox and the other principals were all watching the race. They know what went on.’

Did you see a green bunn-

Can you *please* stop going on about the stupid green bunny?!

Let's hope you don't get locked out before your challenge, Mitch!

I think it'll be very unlikely that I'll be running laps around the school any time soon!

The next day in class ...
Miss, can I go to the toilet please?

Again?!
I think it was some leftover pizza that's done it.

THWAK!

How dare you throw an eraser at me Mitchell! It's detention for you! I shall let Principal Borelock know all about this!
But I ... it wasn't ... I didn't ...

Ahh, back in time for the end of class!
Jai! Mitch's got detention for throwing an eraser at the teacher!
And there's no way he'd have done it!

Mitch wouldn't. But I bet the green bu-

What are you doing lurking around the door?
I just need to get my bag.

Well, hurry up! I better not find you here when I get back from Principal Borelock's office.

Quick, let's rescue Mitch!

C'mon Mitch! We've got to get to the Roblox challenge.
I can't. I have detention. I don't want to get into any more trouble!
But, if we hurry we'll get back here before the teacher returns!
No! I'm not going to risk it!

Ugh! If only Fritz was here to convince you.

C'mon Glitch, let's go. We can't let the academy down!

Fine! If we hurry.

Awesome! Let's go, gang!

Back at the Academy ...
I hope your challengers aren't late again!

No, no. There's our last competitor now.
What!!! He's meant to be in deten ...*cough*I mean, that's good ...

Feel free to start the challenge, Principal Limax, as you do seem fond of pressing buttons.
SLAM!

2ND CHALLENGE - THE PUZZLER

Each player must answer a series of questions as fast as they can. Answer correctly and you advance to the next podium. If you get the answer wrong, or you're too slow, then your podium disappears!

Hey, guys! Your classmate's going well. Keeping up with Gli-

Silence, mammal. We are concentrating.

And with my special machine to focus the minds of the others into hers, she'll be unstoppable!

What is one question that will get different answers at different times and yet would still be correct?
Hmmm, a riddle ...
Question. Sense. Does. Not. Make.
The Slimelox student doesn't look happy.
Neither do her classmates! What's happening to them?
Different times ...
Different answers ...
We! Guess! Confused!

CORRECT! The winner is Glitch and Fritz, from the Academy for Roblox Pros.

Cabbage!

The next morning, Tash, Beatrice, Mitch and Jai chatted happily about the previous day's competition on their way to school.

'I would never have been able to figure that last question out,' said Play.

'Oh, it wasn't that hard. I'm sure you guys would have gotten there in the end,' replied Mitch modestly.

'No way,' said Tash. 'I had no idea!'

'Neither did the Slimelox kid,' added Beatrice. 'Ha! Cabbages!'

‘It’s your challenge today,’ said Mitch. ‘I hope nothing goes wrong for you!’

’What could go wrong?’ replied Beatrice. ‘A forest full of cute animals, me being awesome. Everything will be fine! Unless there are any spiders. Yuck! I can’t stand spiders!’

But something could go very wrong, if you’re being followed by a devious zombie bunny. Little did the friends know that the furry fiend had heard everything, and would soon report it all to the sinister Principal Borelock, A.K.A Principal Limax, A.K.A The Warlock ... who also sometimes goes by the name, Warren.

3RD CHALLENGE- FOREST FRIENDS

Feed and befriend these six forest animals in order.
First to befriend the Golden Bunny. wins!

GO

Bear first ... What do they eat?

Aha! you could help me!
BZZZZZ

BZZZZZZZ

Perfect!

There's a bear already! It must have smelt the honey.

Bear befriended:
2 points

Nom noms! Eat the nom noms you stupid bear!

Deer befriended:
3 points

Squirrel befriended:
5 points

Mouse befriended:
8 points

Sparrow befriended:
13 points

Now to find the golden bunny. I'd better hurry.

Right, I've got a tasty carrot—time to find that bunny.

What's that?

It's the bunny!

Here bunny bunny! I've got a delicious carrot for you!

Why does it keep running away?

Ah! There it is, behind the bush.

Te he he!

I didn't know they had zombie bunnies in the forest. Creepy!

EEEK!

Keep it down! I'm hiding ... I mean, looking for that stupid bear!
S-s-spiders!

We're trapped!

Huh?

It's Uni! She's come to rescue us!
BIFF!
THWACK!

Quick! Get on and let's get out of here!
I'm not getting on that thing!

Suit yourself.
Wait! Don't leave me!
CLIP! CLOP!

Roblox Cup leaderboard:

1. Academy for Roblox Pros (290 points)
2. Slimelox Institute (275 points)
3. Bloxford College (250 points)
4. Obby Academy (230 points)

Later that afternoon at Borelock's ...
You did well in sidetracking Beatrice in the challenge.

But it's not good enough!
We're still behind that fool, Blox, in the points tally!
THWUMP!

We need to take more drastic action ...
pthft!

And I have just the plan!

ZZZZZZ

12:10

No ... urgh ... the green bunny ... zzzz ... the bunnies following me ... mmm pizza ... zzzzzz ...

The next morning at the bus stop ...
Where's Jai? It's his big day today.
BUS STOP
Dunno! Maybe he got a lift to school.
First lesson ...
He's still not here!
This is not good! I'm starting to worry.
Me t-
Shhh! Unless you want detention!
At recess ...
I tried to call him, but there was no answer. Then Principal Borelock came out of his office and shooed me away.
OFFIC

Nooo! Mum! Dad! WAKE UP!

Racing out of the house—then back in again after realising his pants were on backwards—Jai was out of the door in a flash. That is, after one or two pieces of last night's pizza for breakfast—well you can't win the Roblox Cup on an empty stomach!

Panting with exhaustion, and trying to keep the pizza breakfast down, Jai slammed his late note on the school office desk, and pushed his way through the crowds of Borelock's students finishing their lunch.

I can make it! he thought grimly, swallowing hard, as the leftover pizza made another escape attempt.

Once in the lab, he pulled out his special school badge and was once again transported into the Roblox universe.

Yes! I made it!
Um ...
Yeah ...
But the race is almost over, Play.

FINISH

What?! I missed it!

Don't worry, Play. It's only a race. There'll be others.
Sob
sob

I don't care! That green bunny ruined my ...
The green bunny?
Leave it, Bee! I know what I saw.
I know, I saw it too! There was a green zombie bunny in the forest that lead me to the spider trap.
Zombie bunny! Why didn't you tell us before?
I just thought it was part of the game, and then in the excitement of the finish I forgot all about it.

What are you dweebs talking about?!
We think we're being sabotaged in the challenges.
Yeah! By a green bunny!

Green bunny?! You guys are even weirder than those slugs from Slimelox!

Maybe you should ask principal moustache if you can join their school!

Ha! That moustache of his is as ridiculous as Principal Borelock's eyebrows!
Moustache ...
Eyebrows ...
Borelock's ...
Slugs ...
Pizza ...

Are you guys thinking what I'm thinking?
Yep, time for lunch!

No, Play! Principal Limax is Principal Borelock!
And he was also The Warlock and the green zombie bunny is the one Ogre created with the magical staff!
It must have gone back to the real world with Principal Borelock.

He can't be ... *Principal Borelock?* I don't believe it!

Well. There's one way to find out.

Keeping well out of sight, the gang set out after Principal Limax to see if their suspicions were correct.

'Lucky that jacket and hairdo are so bright, otherwise we'd have lost him in the crowds,' whispered Dash.

'Yeah!' agreed Bee in hushed tones. 'Thank goodness for his bad dress sense!'

They continued to follow their (un)fashionable foe away from the other school avatars.

'Where's he going?' asked Fritz.

'I don't know,' replied Glitch. 'But I think we're right. I bet he really is Principal Borelock!'

Just then, Principal Limax stopped and looked around furtively. The kids quickly ducked out of sight and waited.

'He's pulling something out of his jacket,' hissed Play. 'I think it's ... yes, it's an Academy for Roblox Pros school badge! How did he get one of those?

Principal Limax put on the badge, pressed it and disappeared.

I can't believe it!
That was a badge just like ours.
What should we do?
Get back to Borelock's ...
And find out what he's up to.

COMPUTER LAB

EXIT

Look! He's in the school garden.
Maybe he's just hungry?
For cabbages?!

Mmmm! Juicy cabbages ... what a lunch!

What happens now?

I say we charge in and arrest him!

Or, we wait until he leaves, and see what he's up to in there.

A short time later ...
Good, he's leaving.
OK, let's go!

Bio-hazard!
I don't like the sound of that.
Considering how much cabbage he had for lunch, I say we take that warning seriously.
DANGER BIO-HAZARD
KEEP OUT!

Careful! Who knows what's behind the door— it could be poisonous.
Or toxic.
Or worse, a cabbagy principal fart!
Or ...

Slugs!

What the ...
There's hundreds of them!
On tiny computers?!
They're playing Roblox ... These are the Slimelox kids!

You're right! Look, he's made them little name badges and all. Here's Slimone.

Hey, Slimone! It's me, Play.

I think she recognises me!

‘This is astonishing!’ declared Mitch, as he sat down at the main computer. ‘It looks like Principal Borelock has found a way to magnify the slug’s brainwaves!’

‘Surely you can’t boost a slug’s brainwaves enough to match a human,’ said Tash.

Mitch continued, ‘He’s also managed to link all their minds together to create one super slug mind!’

‘What are we going to do?’ asked Beatrice. ‘Slimelox are leading the point tally in the Roblox Cup ...’

‘I don’t want to lose against a bunch of slugs! I say we trash the computer!’ said Jai.

'No, Jai, Principal Borelock will know it was us!' replied Tash urgently. 'We need some other plan. If only we could shut down the program during the team challenge ...'

They all looked at Mitch, who was still investigating the computer system with a look of awe on his face.

'Well, Mitch?' asked Beatrice.

'What? Oh ... maybe. It will be tricky.'

They watched on as Mitch furiously began rewriting the program's code. After a few minutes he leant back and exhaled deeply.

'I think that should do it,' he said hesitantly.

'Quick, let's get out of here before Borelock comes back!' said Tash.

'Good luck at the challenge tomorrow, Slimone,' said Jai, before racing out the door.

Rules of the game:

Each team must defend their flag from the opposing teams, whilst also trying to capture their opponents' flags.

No player is allowed in their own protected area, which is the yellow line around their flag and principal.

Any opposing player that is tagged outside the protected zone, is out of the game.

When a school's flag is taken, all players from that school are out of the game, and their principal is dunked in a vat of slime!

All right! Are all the schools ready?

All set to go!

Ready when you are!

Get on with it Blox!

GO!

Stop! Before we all rush off, we need to make sure we have equal numbers for attack and defence.

We'll go defence. With Fritz's extra eyes, no-one will get past!
I'm going to attack!
Me too!
Then I'll stick in defence with Mitch and Fritz.

Let's keep in touch with a chatbox.
Good idea!
Good luck guys!
You too!

The Bloxford College kids look like they have a good defensive set-up. It'll be hard to get past.
We need some sort of distraction ...

CHAAARGE!

SPLOSH!

That'll do it. Let's go!

Woah!
BOOF!

Oof!
Quietly. Play.
WHAM!

There's the flag, but there's still a lot of defenders in our way. We'll need a plan ...

Got it! We can disguise ourselves as bushes!
Hmmm ... not bad. That might just work. I'll distract the defenders and you creep up to the flag.

Catch me if you can!

Missed me!

OOF!
Oops! My bad!

BLOXFORD FLAG CAPTURED

SPLOSH!

Nice work, Play!

Couldn't have done it without you, Dash!

Dash: We got Bloxford's flag!

Mitch: Awesome

Play: How's it going in defence?

Fritz: We're holding on, and it should get easier now Bloxford are out of the competition.

OBBY ACADEMY FLAG CAPTURED!

With the Obby Academy out of the game, it was now down to the last two schools to battle it out for the win—The Academy for Roblox Pros and the Slimelox Institute.

All was suddenly quiet around the defenders from the Academy of Roblox Pros.

'Right,' said Fritz. 'All we have to do is keep the Slimelox slugs out, till Glitch's program kicks in.'

‘*If* it kicks in,’ said Bee nervously.

‘It’ll work, Bee!’ replied Glitch in a hurt voice. ‘Unless ...’

But a sudden sight over the edge of the hill stopped Glitch’s words in his mouth. From behind every tree and boulder, Slimelox avatars came into view.

‘They’re just standing there, staring,’ muttered Bee.

The Academy kids waited, not sure what to do as the Slimelox students continued to gaze with blank looks on their faces. Then, all at once, and without a word, the Slimelox kids charged.

Fritz: Play, Dash, how's things going for you?

Play: Not good! Arrgh! Almost got me!

Dash: Their ability to share each others minds means we can't get past them!

Dash: And now we're surrounded! When's the program going to work?!

CLICK!

It's worked!
And just in the nick of time!

Look at the Slimelox kids now!
It must be their lunchtime!

Nom! Nom!

Nom! Nom!

Right, there's the Slimelox flag. Let's go get it!

Nom!
Nom!

Watch out!

Where did that come from?
The green bunny!
CRASH!

Leave this one to me ... it's personal now!

C'mon, bunny!
It's time to take
you down!

GRAAARGH!

Owwww!
CHOMP!

Help! Help!
Nice work, Play!
Keep it distracted
and I'll get the flag!

What?! Nooo!
Defend me you
foolish slugs!
Nom!
Nom!

SLIMELOX FLAG CAPTURED

SPLOSH!

We did it!

Good job, your program worked, Glitch.
Of course ... I wasn't worried at all.
Ha!

Where's Play?

I'm here ... Is the bunny gone?
Not a bunny in sight. But there is a nice shiny gold cup!

Well done, everyone! What a great competition!

And a special thanks for sparing me a slime bath.

SLOOP!
Cheats! Sabotage! Gimme that cup! I demand a ...
SQUELCH!

OOF!
SPLAT!

Principal Limax! Calm down.

Principal Limax?! That's not who I am. Don't you recognise me? It is I ...

The Warlock!

Um ... Your eyebrows are upside-down.
We know.

You meddling children may have foiled me again ...

But it's not the last you'll see of me!

Well duh! We'll see him at Borelock's.

They watched The Warlock run hysterically off into the distance, before joining the rest of their schoolmates to celebrate the victory. They talked, laughed, carried around the cup and much to Play's delight, ate pizza.

Just before they were due to return to Borelock's, Principal Blox came up to talk to them. 'So, you know our good friend, the Warlock?' he asked.

'Yep,' replied Bee. 'We're lucky enough to have him as our principal back in the real world. And in case you're wondering, his dress sense is just as bad there, too!'

‘He must have gotten into the Roblox universe when we were sucked in the first time,’ said Mitch. ‘I guess the portal stayed open after we slipped through. We are so sorry!’

‘Don’t be!’ laughed Principal Blox. ‘He’s made this year’s Roblox Cup the most exciting that it’s been in a long time! My only worry is how you’re going to be able to deal with him in the real world,’ continued the principal. ‘He must be a cunning genius to do all he’s done in Roblox.’

‘Ummm ... If he is, he’s hiding it very well,’ replied Dash.

Well kids, it sounds like you have a lot on your hands with that principal, but I'm sure you can handle it.

Thanks, Principal Blox.

Yeah, we'll be fine.

We've already thwarted him twice.

Well, time to get back to Borelock's.

I guess the fun has to end some time.

C'mon guys, we've got the inter-school cup to compete in!

Oh ...yay.

It might be different this time. We just need to treat it like a Roblox challenge!

What, like one that's being sabotaged by an evil warlock?

The next day it was time for Borelock's Academy to compete in the annual district inter-school cup.

There were sporting challenges, math and science competitions and even a pizza eating contest. Beatrice, Mitch, Tash and Jai, fresh from their Roblox Cup win, threw themselves into the challenges with renewed enthusiasm—though

Jai would have happily eaten loads of pizza any day!

The rest of the Borelock's students, seeing their friends' efforts, also tried harder than ever before.

At the end of the day, all the schools gathered together to hear who'd won the overall competition.

I have the final points tally here, and it's my pleasure to announce that this year's winner is ...

WOO!
YAY!
CHEER!
1st
CLAP!
CLAP!
CLAP!

I ... I ... I won?
I finally won!

cough I mean ... congratulations, Borelock's students! I'm so proud of what you've achieved.
1st

Wow! That's the first positive thing I've ever heard him say.
Is that really Principal Borelock?

Later, at the end of the day ...
Hey, Principal Warlo ... Borelock! The trophy looks nice, doesn't it?

Huh? What? Oh. It's you four.

Yes, it does look rather splendid!

He was smiling ... actually smiling!
I know! Creepy ...
Hey, guys! Look who it is!

I wonder what adventures we have in store for us next week?

More principal thwarting, no doubt.

I don't know. I think Principal Borelock's turned over a new leaf ...

Meanwhile, in Roblox ...
Ah, Borelock ... or should I say, Warlock. I've summoned you back because I'm a little disappointed with you.

First, you lose the magic wand I gave you, and now this! I give you the technology to make a school of super avatars, and you fail me again!

Maybe the bunny should be my chosen henchman instead ...

Anything would be better than you, it seems! However, I do have another job for you ...

B-b-but,your lordship, I've been doing some thinking and I don't want to be the Warlock anymore. I just want to enjoy Roblox and ...

The Robug!

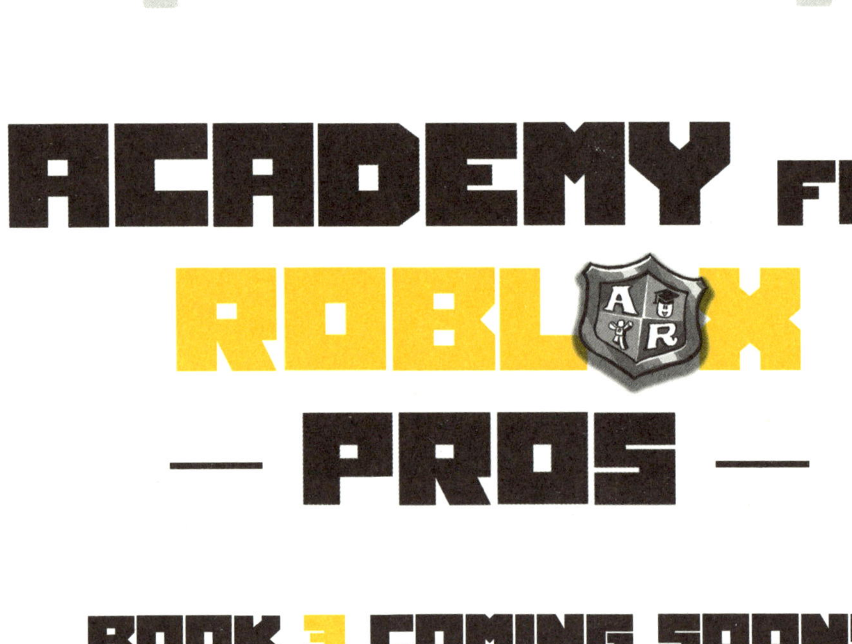

BOOK 3 COMING SOON!